How Well Do You Know The Black History of Natchez, Mississippi?

By: Jeremy Houston

To: David & Joy

From: Jeremy Houston

Thanks for your support & care for Natchez History

JxH 3/23/2019

Copyright © 2017 Jeremy Houston

All rights reserved.

ISBN:172956593X
ISBN-13: 978-1729565933

DEDICATION

ANTHONY HAYWOOD
BOBBY BUTLER
MILDRED JEAN WILSON
RODNEY GRAY
JARED FORD
JESSIE TAYLOR JR.
CLARENCE A. MCQUARTERS
JOHNNY FRANKLIN
KENDRICK TOLBERT
CHAVARIS MARTIN
CEDRIC MORGAN
CLIFTON JACKSON
TIMOTHY O'NEAL
TERRANCE THORNBURG
DAMIEN GREEN
KEVIN SADLER
DSHUN WATSON
ESTHER REASON
CEDRIC ANDERSON
DEREK "BIG RED" JARVIS
ASHLEY MARSAW
And to all who transitioned to the next life.
REST IN POWER FOREVER!

TABLE OF CONTENTS

	About The Author	I
1	The Bambara & Natchez Massacre	Pg 8
2	Abd Al- Rahman Ibrahim Ibn Sori	Pg 9
3	Forks of The Road Slave Market	Pg 11
4	The Murder of Duncan Skinner	Pg 13
5	Free People of Color In Antebellum Natchez	Pg 14
6	Civil War 1861-1865	Pg 16
7	Reconstruction	Pg 18
8	Jim Crow & Natchez Civil Rights Movement	Pg 20
9	Modern Times In Natchez	Pg 26
Quiz:	How Well Do You Know The Black History of Natchez?	Pg 28

ABOUT THE AUTHOR

Jeremy Houston is the grandson of Freeman and Esther Reason and son of Alvin and Theresa Houston. Jeremy was born on December 25, 1987, in Natchez, Mississippi. He was reared at a young age by his parents, grandparents, close relatives, and the community of Minorville.
He graduated from Natchez High School in 2006. Upon graduation, he attended Northeast Mississippi Community College on a basketball scholarship. After one season in college, he decided to join the United States Marine Corps. While in the Marines, he deployed to Afghanistan, Japan, Thailand, Kenya and countless other locations on the globe. Also he played organized basketball in across the United States and the world.
After five years of service to the Marines, He moved back to Natchez in 2012. Immediately, he connected with Ser Seshs-Boxley and Darrell White to begin working on the Equalization of Natchez History concerning people or African descent or black people in Natchez and the surrounding areas. Groups like the National Black United Front, New Black Panther Party, National of Islam under the Honorable Louis Farrakhan, and the Ethiopian World Federation are some of the national groups that have worked with him and others in Natchez. In 2016, Jeremy Houston ran for Alderman of Ward 4 in Natchez. His campaign motto was "ONE WARD! ONE AIM! ONE DESTINY! Also that year, the Miss Lou Heritage Group & Tours LLC was established by Houston and Bryan Mcknight.
"When we all wake up and realize that we must put aside our petty differences and learn to agree to disagree on small matters. We will go to a level Natchez has never seen before."- Jeremy Houston

The 1st Enslaved Africans In Natchez

CHAPTER 1
THE BAMBARA & NATCHEZ MASSACRE

The Bambara Nation of Mali are the 1st known Africans to be enslaved in Natchez by the French in 1719.
    The Bambara are sometimes called the Bamana people. The Bambara traditionally worshipped one God
they called Bemba or Ngala.
The Bambara were known for their agricultural skills which contributed to the development of Natchez. The French traded in slaves and brought the first African slaves to Natchez to cultivate tobacco.

One of the earliest recorded incidents of a slave uprising in the area was the Natchez Indian Revolt of 1729 against the French colonists. The Bambara were known as a militant group of people. Sparked by the Natchez Indians in protest of cruelty by French, Natchez Indians recruited several Bambara, promising them freedom, and staged a revolt against the French, wherein approximately 230 people were killed. The French retaliated, using their allies from other Indian tribes to punish the Natchez, and recovered many of the enslaved. The Natchez Indians ultimately lost the war.

CHAPTER 2
ABD AL-RAHMAN IBRAHIMA IBN SORI
"PRINCE AMONG SLAVES"

Born a Prince in 1762 near Timbuktu, Abd al-Rahman Ibrahima was the son of Sori, King of the Fulbe empire. Abd al-Rahman Ibrahima was educated at the University in Timbuktu. In 1788, while in battle with his father's army, Ibrahima was captured. He was sold into slavery and brought to Natchez where he was sold to planter Thomas Foster. In 1794 he married Isabella, another one slave of Foster's, and eventually fathered a large family: five sons and four daughters.

In 1807, while at the market, Ibrahima was recognized by Dr. John Cox, whose life had been saved in Africa by Ibrahima's father. Dr. Cox immediately began efforts to obtain Ibrahima's freedom. Dr. Cox would die before Ibrahima would obtain freedom. Dr. Cox's son would take up where his father left off and helped obtained Ibrahima and his wife's freedom. Though Foster freed Ibrahima, he couldn't live in America as a free man could. Before leaving the U.S., Abdul-Rahman and his wife went to various states and Washington, D.C. where he met with President Adams in person. He solicited donations, through the press, personal appearances, the American Colonization Society and politicians, to free his family back in Mississippi. Abdul-Rahman's actions and freedom were also used against President John Quincy Adams by future president Andrew Jackson during the presidential election. After ten months of freedom in the U.S., Ibrahima returned to Africa but died in Liberia before making it back to his homeland of Timbo. Ibrahima and Isabella only raised half of the funds to free two sons and their families. In 1977, history professor Terry Alford documented the life of Ibrahima in his ground-breaking book Prince Among Slaves, the first full account of his life, pieced together from first-person accounts and historical documents.

In 2006, Abdul-Rahman's descendants from Liberia and the United States gathered for a family reunion in Natchez, Mississippi at Foster's Field.

CHAPTER 3
THE FORKS OF THE ROAD SLAVE MARKET

As the cotton business grows in Natchez, the need for a labor force became high demand. "BUY MORE NEGROES TO RAISE MORE COTTON TO BUY MORE NEGROES" becomes one of the mottos the wealthy planters in Natchez. In 1833, the Forks of The Road, named for the conversion point of three major roads leading into the city of Natchez, began operating as a domestic market place for selling of enslaved Africans. Enslavement dealers at the Forks of the Road used the Natchez newspapers to announce the availability of slaves for purchase, indicating a casual, first-come-first-served approach to marketing slaves. Dealers such as R.H. Elam, Thomas G. James, Griffin & Pullum, Theophilus Freeman, and the most notorious of them all Isaac Franklin and John Armfield of 1315 Duke Street, Alexandria, Virginia made a fortune off the selling of enslaved Africans. At the Forks of the Road, thousands of enslaved Africans were walked, sailed, bought, and sold in support of the cotton business in Natchez. The Forks of the Road was not an auction but that similar to a modern day car dealership. The men, women, and children would be separated. The men would be dressed in fine suites and hats and women dressed in nice hoop skirts. Also greasy pot liquor was applied to the bodies of the enslaved to increase the value of their sale. New England writer Joseph Holt Ingraham, who visited the Forks of the Road slave market about 1834, wrote, "Slaves at the Forks of the Road are not sold at auction, or all at once, but singly, or in parties, as purchasers may be inclined to buy." By early 1850, male slaves at Forks of the Road were advertised at $825 each, and females were priced at $700 and $600. By early 1861, with a civil war looming, prices for Virginia field hand slaves had climbed to an average of $1,200 each. The last sales of the enslaved Africans at the Forks of the Road happened in early 1863.

By July 13, 1863, the Union Army invades Natchez with 5,000 troops. Of which 3,000 were of the newly formed United States Colored Troops (USCT). At the Forks of the Road, the USCT built barracks and used the area as a recruitment center for newly emancipated African people. In modern times in Natchez, Ser Seshs Ab Heter- C.M. Boxley has led successful efforts on the development of the Forks of the Road Historic Slave Market as a National Historic Landmark for the history of the domestic slave trade in America.

CHAPTER 4
THE MURDER OF DUNCAN SKINNER 1857

In 1857, Duncan Skinner, a cruel and vicious white overseer of Clarissa Sharpe's Cedar Grove Plantation southeast Natchez, is found dead in the woods of the plantation. Duncan Skinner was a notoriously violent overseer who flailed slaves at Bon Ridge every evening. Overseeing was a demanding job. It involved supervising the work of slaves, monitoring what they did in their spare time, and, in many instances, taking part in the financial operations of the plantation. It was Duncan's brother, Jesse, who was working as overseer on nearby Smithland plantation, who first raised questions about the verdict of accidental death. Initially some thought Skinner had fell from his horse, but after further investigation by Skinner's brother Jesse and area planters came to the conclusion that foul play was involved. Three slaves named Anderson, Rueben, and Henderson of the Cedar Grove Plantation abducted Skinner and killed him in the nearby woods. Soon after, they cleverly crafted the scene of a riding accident using Skinners body, his belongings, and a horse. The planters immediately rounded up the Cedar Groves slaves and forced them not only to confess to the murder, but to also falsely implicate a white carpenter, John McCallin, as instigator of the killing. McCallin eventually was found guilty of lying and complicity but was forced to leave town. Henderson, Rueben, and Anderson were charged and hung for the murder of the brutal overseer.

CHAPTER 5
FREE PEOPLE OF COLOR IN ANTEBELLUM NATCHEZ

Natchez's free people of color enjoyed exceptional privileges. They were literate, owned property and slaves, and had their marriages officially recorded. In manners and deportment they emulated the white planter aristocracy and stood aloof socially from slaves and lower class free blacks. They viewed with disdain what they considered the uncouth behavior of the lower classes, both black and white. Their keen sense of propriety prompted them to look upon "darkey parties" in which slaves and lower class free blacks intermingled socially as amusements of too low minded wretches.

ROBERT McCARY
Born a slave, was freed, along with his sister, in 1815 by the will of their father. Both siblings inherited town lots in Natchez and received income from the labor of two slaves. As an adult, McCary became a barber, acquired real estate, owned slaves, and purchased stock in the Mississippi Railroad Company.

WILLIAM McCARY
Son of Robert McCary, a prominent black of the Natchez community during Reconstruction, served as city alderman, county treasurer, sheriff, and postmaster of Natchez.

ROBERT SMITH
Born a free person of color in Maryland. In the 1830's Smith owned and operated a grocery store in New Orleans. While in New Orleans, Smith bought and sold property and even buys slaves. Smith purchased Annette McCauley and gave her freedom. According to the state of Louisiana, once an enslaved person freedom was purchased, that person had to leave the state. Smith moved to Natchez. Prohibited from operating a store in Mississippi, Smith started a successful hack (taxi) service in the city of Natchez. Smith would go on to marry McCauley in Natchez. Robert Smith died in 1858. The local newspaper described Smith as having "won the favor and respect of the entire community." His

HOW WELL DO YOU KNOW THE BLACK HISTORY OF NATCHEZ, MISSISSIPPI?

wife became the first woman of color to operate a significant business in the city's history after his death. After racial and economic tensions began to rise, she moved to Valparaiso Chile before the Civil War.

WILLIAM JOHNSON

Born a slave in 1809, Johnson received his freedom in 1820 from his owner and father. His mother Amy had been freed in 1814 and his sister Adelia in 1818. As a youth, Johnson trained to be a barber with his brother-in-law, James Miller. As a adult, Johnson became a successful entrepreneur with a barbershop, bath house, and land holdings throughout the region. Johnson also owned sixteen slaves. In 1835, he married Ann Battle; the couple had eleven children. Johnson loaned money to many people and wrote a daily diary of his life. That gave an account of how free people of color lived in antebellum Natchez.

In 1851, Johnson had a land disputes with Baylor Winn. This led to the two men in court. Although, the judge ruled in Johnson's favor, Winn was not satisfied. Winn, also a free black ambushed Johnson returning from his farm and shot him. Johnson lived long enough to name Winn as the person who shot him. Through strange circumstances, Winn was never convicted of the killing. Winn and his defense argued that he was actually white and not a free person of color because of his Indian ancestry in Virginia. Mississippi law allowed for blacks to testify against whites in civil cases, but not in criminal cases. Two hung juries could not decide if he was white or black, so Johnson's Killer walked free. Johnson's diary was rediscovered in 1938 and published in 1951. It reveals much of the daily life of a 19th-century Mississippi businessman, including the fact that he was himself later a slaveholder. His papers are archived at Louisiana State University. Johnson's house on State Street in downtown Natchez continued to be owned by the family until they sold it to the Ellicott Hill Preservation Society in 1976. The house was then donated to the city who in turn donated to the National Park Service in 1990. After an extensive restoration process, the National Park Service opened the house as a museum detailing Johnson's life in 2005.

CHAPTER 6
CIVIL WAR 1861-1865

The United States Colored Troops Presence in the Miss Lou Area. The selling of enslaved Africans ceased in Natchez by the summer of 1863 when Union troops occupied the town. In July 1863, General Walter Gresham and five thousand Union Army Soldiers of which three thousand were of the newly formed United States Colored Troops (USCT). The 58th Regiment, United States Colored Infantry, 71st United States Colored Infantry Regiment, & the 6th Regiment, United States Colored Heavy Artillery were some of the USCT Units stationed in Natchez during the Civil War. African American troops fought valiantly in the Civil War. Fort McPherson, in Natchez, Mississippi, was a Civil War fort built primarily by United States Colored Troops (USCT). Fort McPherson and the Forks of the Road became a major recruiting center for the USCT, which was comprised especially of African American slaves who ran away from the places where they had been held in bondage. Together, these two sites, located on opposite ends of Natchez. Self-emancipation and active resistance by African Americans was what changed the landscape of the war.

WILSON BROWN
Born 1841 as a slave in Natchez, Mississippi. In 1863, Brown enlisted in the Union Navy and was assigned as a landsman to the USS Hartford. On August 5, 1864, during the Battle of Mobile Bay, as the squadron came under fire from Fort Morgan, Fort Gaines, and Confederate ships. Brown and a group sailors worked on the Hartford's berth deck loading gunpowder up to the gun deck. As they worked, a Confederate shell exploded in their midst. Brown was blown through a hatch and landed unconscious on the deck below; the dead body of another man landed on top of him. The only other of the six men to survive was Landsman John Lawson, who was thrown against a bulkhead and momentarily stunned. After regaining consciousness, Brown and Lawson

HOW WELL DO YOU KNOW THE BLACK HISTORY OF NATCHEZ, MISSISSIPPI?

continued in their duties, keeping the ship's guns supplied with powder, through the remainder of the battle.

For these actions, both Brown and Lawson were awarded the Medal of Honor four months later, on December 31, 1864.

Landsman Brown's official Medal of Honor citation reads:

On board the flagship U.S.S. Hartford during successful attacks against Fort Morgan, rebel gunboats and the ram CSS Tennessee in Mobile Bay on 5 August 1864. Knocked unconscious into the hold of the ship when an enemy shell burst fatally wounded a man on the ladder above him, Brown, upon regaining consciousness, promptly returned to the shell whip on the berth deck and zealously continued to perform his duties although 4 of the 6 men at this station had been either killed or wounded by the enemy's terrific fire.

CHAPTER 7
RECONSTRUCTION

ROBERT WOOD
Born 1844 to Susie Harris, a black house servant and Dr. Robert Wood, a white doctor from Virginia. Wood's parents never married but lived side by side. Wood was never a slave and lived mostly with his father, former mayor of Natchez. In 1869, Mississippi Governor James L. Alcorn appointed Robert Wood as mayor of Natchez, Mississippi. Making Wood the first person of African descent to hold the office of Mayor in Natchez. He was elected mayor in 1870. Wood's election was part of the "Black and Tan Revolution," a short-lived political shift in Mississippi. As mayor, Wood built Natchez's first school for African Americans (Union Street School) in 1871. Prior to Wood's political career, he worked as a printer at Natchez printing company. After his term as mayor of Natchez, Wood served as postmaster and tax collector for the city of Natchez. In 1875, Wood was elected Sheriff of Adams County, Mississippi. After his political work, Wood operated a store in Washington, Mississippi, three miles north of Natchez. Wood's descendants are the Mackel Family who own and operate one of the oldest funeral homes in the state of Mississippi.

LOUIS J. WINSTON
Born 1844 to a prominent planter and enslaved mother. During the period of Reconstruction, Winston served as a policeman, sheriff, tax assessor, and clerk of court. Winston was also a practicing attorney and planter. Winston founded the Colored Building and Loan Association, which financed the sales of new homes to people of African descent. He also served as manager for the Mississippi Cooperative and Benefit Association. In 1918 Louis Winston died in Lexington, Mississippi. The Woodmen of the Union honored Winston as their founder by commissioning the bronze bust on his tombstone. Winston's grave is the only grave with a bronze bust in the Natchez City Cemetery.

HOW WELL DO YOU KNOW THE BLACK HISTORY OF NATCHEZ, MISSISSIPPI?

JOHN ROY LYNCH

Born a slave in 1847, on the Tacony Plantation in Vidalia, Louisiana. Lynch's parents were Catherine White, who was enslaved and Patrick Lynch, an Irish immigrant. After Lynch's father death, he and his family were sold to the Dunleith Plantation in Natchez. Lynch remained a slave until 1863. After the Civil War, Lynch became one of the most powerful political figures in America. He first appointed Justice of the Peace in Adams County. By 1869, he was elected to the Mississippi Legislature. Lynch became the first person of African descent to serve as Speaker of the House. At the age of 25, he was elected to the first of three successful terms as a congressman representing Adams County. In 1884 Lynch was appointed by future president Theodore Roosevelt as temporary chairman of the Republican National Convention. This made him the first person of African descent in the United States to chair a national political convention. In 1896 he was admitted to the Mississippi Bar Association. In 1901 he served as paymaster of the Army. Lynch moved to Chicago in 1912. He practiced law there until his death in 1939.

HIRAM RHODES REVELS

Born a free man in North Carolina in 1827. Revels was a minister in the African Methodist Episcopal Church (AME), a Republican politician, and college administrator. In 1868, while the pastor of Zion Chapel AME Church, he served as one of the first black alderman in the city of Natchez. In 1870 Revels was elected by a vote of 81 to 15 in the Mississippi State Senate to finish the term of one of the state's two seats in the US Senate, which had been left vacant since the Civil War. Previously, it had been held by Jefferson Davis, who was the president of the Confederacy. After one year as a senator, Revels resigned and became president of the first land grant college in Mississippi for the education of newly emancipated, Alcorn College. Revels also served as Secretary of State in Mississippi. Revels died in 1901 in Aberdeen, Mississippi. He is buried at the Hillcrest Cemetery in Holly Springs, Mississippi.

CHAPTER 8
JIM CROW
AND
THE NATCHEZ CIVIL RIGHTS MOVEMENT

The UNIA IN NATCHEZ
In the 1920s the movement of Black Nationalist and Pan Africanist, Marcus Garvey came to Natchez, Mississippi. Garveyism had a strong appeal in Natchez. The editor of the Natchez Democrat recognized the popularity of the UNIA and Negro World in the Deep South primarily in Natchez. At the 1924 convention of the UNIA, Natchez minister Reverend R.H. Cosgrove reported every member of his 500 member church was a member of the UNIA. Cosgrove attended the convention to see things for himself so that he could take back to the people who trusted him a true report of work of the movement.
In 1929, Reverend G.C. Ford of Natchez attended the 6th International UNIA Convention in Kingston, Jamaica with Marcus Garvey. The UNIA would have a presence in Natchez well into the 1940s. In 2015, Jeremy Houston and the Miss Lou Heritage Group & Tours celebrated the 1st Marcus Garvey Day in Natchez, Mississippi.

THE RHYTHM CLUB FIRE
On April 23,1940 209 African Americans perished in one of the deadliest night club fires in American history. The local Moneywasters Social Club brought Walter Barnes and Orchestra to Natchez for a one night performance. The news of Barnes coming to town spread like wild fire. This led the Moneywasters Social Club to board the windows to prevent outsiders from viewing or listening to the music, the crowd was literally trapped. Around 11:30 PM the fire began at the main entrance door. The fire spread quickly throughout the building, due to Spanish Moss sprayed with a pesticide named Flit. More than 300 people struggled to get out after the blaze began. A handful of people were able to get out the front door or through the ticket booth, while the remainder tried to press their way to the back door which was padlocked and boarded shut. Blinding smoke made movement difficult.

HOW WELL DO YOU KNOW THE BLACK HISTORY OF NATCHEZ, MISSISSIPPI?

Many people died from smoke inhalation or trampling by the crowd trying to escape. The day after the blaze, five men were arrested after reports they had drunkenly threatened in an argument to burn the building down. Charges against them were later dropped. In the aftermath of the fire, bodies that couldn't be recognized by family or members of the community, were buried in a mass grave at the city's local Colored cemetery. Citizens of Natchez raised more than $5,000 to help the local Red Cross in relief efforts. Because of this fire, fire codes in America were changed. This fire not only affected the city of Natchez in 1940 but for future generations to come. The disaster was memorialized in songs such as "The Death of Walter Barnes" by Leonard Caston; "The Natchez Burnin" by Howlin' Wolf; and "Natchez Fire" by John Lee Hooker. In 2010, Monroe and Betty Sago opened the Rhythm Club Museum, a museum dedicated to commemorating the tragedy in Natchez.

RICHARD WRIGHT

Born in 1908 near Natchez. Wright was the son of Nathan Wright and Ella Wilson. Wright's grandfathers had taken part in the US Civil War: his paternal grandfather Nathan Wright (1842–1904) had served in the 58th USCT, while his maternal grandfather Richard Wilson (1847–1921) was an escaped slave who served in the US Navy as a Landsman in April 1865. Wright's father left the family when he was young boy. In 1923, Wright who had excelled in grade school and then junior high school, and was made class valedictorian of Smith Robertson School in Jackson, Mississippi. Wright moved to Chicago in 1927, an began working as a postal clerk. By 1932, began attending meetings held by the Communist Party. Wright had completed his first novel,
Cesspool. Cesspool would not be published until after his death in 1963. In 1937, Richard Wright moved to New York, where he forged new ties with Communist Party members. Wright gained national attention for the collection of four short stories entitled Uncle Tom's Children(1938). He based some stories on lynching in the Deep South. In 1940, Wright's book Native Son was released. In January 1941 Wright received the prestigious Spingarn Medal for noteworthy achievement by a black. Wright's semi-autobiographical

Black Boy (1945) described his early life from Roxie up until his move to Chicago at age 19, his clashes with his Seventh-day Adventist family, his troubles with white employers and social isolation. Wright moved to Paris in 1946, and became a permanent American expatriate. The FBI had Wright under surveillance starting in 1943. Wright was blacklisted by Hollywood movie studio executives in the 1950s, but, in 1950, starred as the teenager Bigger Thomas (Wright was 42) in an Argentinian film version of Native Son. In 1954, Wright's book Black Power is published. Black Power was inspired by his visit to the Gold Coast the year before.
Other works by Richard Wright included White Man, Listen! (1957); a novel The Long Dream in 1958.
Wright died of heart attack, in 1960, while living in Paris France. He was interred in Le Père Lachaise
Cemetery. In 2008, portion of US Highway 84 located in Adams County is named the Richard Wright
Memorial Highway.

GEORGE METCALFE

Born in 1911. Metcalfe was a civil rights leader who became the President of the Natchez chapter of the NAACP and treasurer of the Jackson, Mississippi chapter of the NAACP in the mid 1960's. On August 19,1965, Metcalfe began campaigning to end school segregation and submitted a petition to the school board. He also submitted requests to not release the names of those who signed the petition but the press released them anyway. In August of 1965, Metcalfe who was employed at Armstrong Tire and Rubber Company, was bombed in the parking lot of the plant. Miraculously, Metcalfe survived despite extensive injuries. Aftermath included federal troops dispatched to Natchez to control the threat of riot. Metcalfe's bombing led to a series of events that changed Natchez racial climate forever. Metcalfe died in 1989 and is buried near Monroe, Louisiana.

The 1965 PARCHMAN ORDEAL

In the aftermath of the 1965 bombing of George Metcalfe, hundreds of the black community in Natchez organized to bring an end to segregation. In early October of 1965, approximately 700

HOW WELL DO YOU KNOW THE BLACK HISTORY OF NATCHEZ, MISSISSIPPI?

black citizens were congregated and arrested at the city's auditorium. They were all arrested for Parading Without A Permit. Two hundred of those who were arrested were shipped off in buses to Parchman (Mississippi State Penitentiary) where they subjected to vicious mistreatment and abuse. None of these individuals ever went before a judge or had a day in court. Individuals like Wharlest Jackson Sr., George F. West Sr., and Nellie Jackson spearheaded efforts in bailing out and bringing the protesters home from Parchman. In 2013, Ser Seshs Ab Heter and Darrell White led efforts to recognize the work and sacrifices of those individuals who were sent to Parchman.
In 2015, after 50 years of injustice, the city of Natchez publicly apologized to the individuals involved in the Parchman Ordeal. Former Natchez Mayor Larry "Butch" Brown quoted, "The city of Natchez must stare down its shame for the mistreatment of hundreds of innocent, black Natchezians. Even though it has been a long time coming, it is not too late to recognize and apologize to those true heroes of Natchez who bravely endured degradation in advancing the cause of equality before the law." A film titled "The Parchman Ordeal: The Untold Story" was released in 2016 detailing the stories of people from Natchez, who were sent to Parchman in 1965.

WILLIAM "BILL" WARE

Born 1935 in Adams County. Bill Ware was raised by his paternal grandparents, who worked as sharecroppers. Highly educated and a veteran of the US Army, Ware understood the climate of racism in the JIM CROW south. In 1963 as a member of SNCC (Student Nonviolent Coordinating Committee) is brutally beaten and arrested in Natchez for using a white restroom. This made Bill Ware the first person to be arrested for civil rights in Natchez. While at the hospital receiving stitches for his wounds, the physician called Ware brainwashed and had no respect for the southern way of life. Though he recovered from his physical wounds, the mental wounds would remain for the rest of his life In the 1965 movie "Black Natchez", Ware is the tall young man standing on top of a car in front of the then NAACP headquarters urging blacks to march on city hall. After the civil rights movement Ware became active in other movements across the country. In

2014, Ware died in Natchez, Mississippi. Ware's legacy to Natchez will always be remembered in Natchez as one who was not scared to speak up in a time of despair.

WHARLEST JACKSON

Born February 7, 1930, Wharlest Jackson was a Korean War veteran, married with five children, who worked the Armstrong Tire and Rubber Company with George Metcalfe (Natchez NAACP President), and treasurer of Natchez chapter of the NAACP. After working close hand to hand with George Metcalfe on issues of civil rights in Natchez, Wharlest Jackson became a target for the local faction of the KKK, the Silver Dollar Group. The 1965 bombing of George Metcalfe led Jackson to enhance his efforts in the quest for equality in Natchez. In 1967, Jackson took a position as a chemical mixer at Armstrong. Because of this decision and the racial climate at the plant, Jackson's family knew it was a matter of time before he would experience backlash for accepting this position. On February 27, 1967, Jackson who
finished his normal shift was asked to work overtime. Tired from working his previous shift, Jackson reluctantly worked the shift and prepared to go home. Jackson started his truck and drove down Minor Street. At the corner of Minor and Henderson Streets, Jackson's truck exploded, killing him instantly. Until this date, no one has ever been prosecuted for his death. The Miss Lou Heritage Group & Tours commemorates Wharlest Jackson by growing a community garden in his honor.

NATCHEZ RIOT OF 1968

In 1968 tensions locally and nationally between blacks and whites grew to an all time high. This led to nationwide protests and riots. Natchez would follow as in June of 1968, a riot ensued. The riot started on St. Catherine Street and then Pine Street with a altercation between a black man and a white gas station
owner. According to Mr. Earl Johnson of Natchez, who was a young man at the time said, "When we heard the news of what happened, immediately we called up our people in Natchez and Vidalia, Louisiana. Together we organized and took over control of the city from the police in Natchez." The riot resulted in store fires along Pine Street and St. Catherine Street with white store owners

HOW WELL DO YOU KNOW THE BLACK HISTORY OF NATCHEZ, MISSISSIPPI?

reportedly shooting at black activists. The National Guard managed to take back control of the city. The Black leaders of Natchez didn't want to meet with Mayor John Nosser because of their distrust with him. Future Mayor Tony Byrne and Civil Rights Activist Charles Evers met with the black leaders at the city's chamber to calm everyone down. The riot led many people in the community to look for solutions to end hatred and fear between blacks and whites in Natchez. The riot also led to blacks moving up the social ladder in society in Natchez.

CHAPTER 9
MODERN TIMES IN NATCHEZ

Barney Schoby Sr.
The first black elected to the Adams County Board Supervisors since Reconstruction.

Phillip West
In 2004, West became the first black man elected to the office of mayor in Natchez since Reconstruction.
West also served on the Adams County Board of Supervisors and Mississippi House of Representatives.

Mary Lee Toles
The first black female to serve as Judge in Adams County Justice Court and also served as an
Alderwoman for the city of Natchez.

Travis L. Patten
Educated in the Natchez-Adams School District. Patten served in the US Navy and as a police officer in
Natchez. In 2015, Patten was elected as the first black sheriff in Adams County since Reconstruction.

Je'Kel Foster
A Professional basketball player in Europe born in Natchez. In 2009, Foster helped lead EWE Baskets
Oldenburg to the German League championship title. In 2007 and 2012, Foster was named a German
League All Star.

HOW WELL DO YOU KNOW THE BLACK HISTORY OF NATCHEZ, MISSISSIPPI?

Steven Ridley

Born in Natchez, Mississippi. In 2007 while attending Louisiana State University (LSU) Ridley won a
BCS National College Football Championship. Ridley was drafted by the New England Patriots in 2011.
In 2015, Ridley won a NFL Super Bowl Championship.

HOW WELL DO YOU KNOW THE BLACK HISTORY OF NATCHEZ? QUIZ

This is a twenty multiple choice questions quiz on the Black History of Natchez . Test your knowledge and see How Well Do You Know The Black History of Natchez, Mississippi?

Question 1:
Who were the first people of African descent to be brought to Natchez as slaves in 1719?
A. The Bambara
B. The Chokwe
C. The Zulus
D. The Dogon

Question 2:
What year did the Forks of the Road Slave Market come into existence?
A.   1835
B.   1845
C.   1833
D.   1861

Question 3:
Which of the following individuals was the President of the Natchez Chapter of the NAACP in 1965?
A.   George Metcalfe
B.   Archie Curtis
C.   Wharlest Jackson
D.   James Jackson

Question 4:
What was the name of the nightclub in which 209 African Americans perished on April 23, 1940?
A. Cotton Club
B. Rhythm Club
C. The Palace
D. Jack's Place

HOW WELL DO YOU KNOW THE BLACK HISTORY OF NATCHEZ, MISSISSIPPI?

Question 5:
Who was the performing band at The Rhythm Nightclub on the night of April 23, 1940?
A. Duke Ellington
B. Billie Holiday
C. Walter Barnes and Orchestra
D. Bud Scott's Band

Question 6:
What is the name of the church that Hiram R. Revels pastored in Natchez?
A.   Rose Hill Baptist Church
B.   Zion Chapel A.M.E. Church
C.   Beulah Baptist Church
D.   Mount Sinai Baptist Church

Question 7:
Who was the first person arrested for civil rights movement in Natchez?
A.   John Lewis
B.   George F West
C.   Sadie V Thompson
D.   William "Bill" Ware

Question 8:
Who is Winston Hill in Natchez named after?
A.   Louis Winston
B.   George Washington Brumfield
C.   John R. Lynch
D.   Robert Scott

Question 9:
Who was the black United States congressman from Adams County during Reconstruction?
A. Robert B. Elliot
B. John R. Lynch
C. PBS Pinchbach
D. William Alexander

Question 10:
Who is the first person of African descent to hold the office of Mayor in the city of Natchez?
A. John Banks
B. Dr. Albert Dumas
C. Robert Wood
D. Dr. Michael Turner

Question 11:
In what year did Steven Ridley win a NFL Superbowl Championship?
2001
B. 1943
C. 1919
D. 2015

Question 12:
In what year did the Forks of the Road Slave Market cease to exist as a market?
1863
1888
1823
1856

Question 13:
In what year did the Natchez Riot happen?
A. 1945
B. 1960
C. 1968
D. 1999

HOW WELL DO YOU KNOW THE BLACK HISTORY OF NATCHEZ, MISSISSIPPI?

Questions 14:
Which two free people of color worked as barbers in Antebellum Natchez ?
A. George Washington Brumfield
B. Robert McCary
C. William Johnson
D. Both B & C

Question 15:
Where was Abd al-Rahman Ibrahima Ibn Sori educated?
A. Alcorn State University
B. University in Timbuktu
C. Jackson, Mississippi
D. Ethiopia

Question 16:
Who is the first black sheriff elected in Adams County since Reconstruction?
A. Travis Patten
B. Billy Thomas
C. Michael King
D. Robert Wood

Question 17:
In which book did Richard Wright give an account of his life in Mississippi?
A. Native Son
B. Lawd Today
C. Green Eggs and Ham
D. Black Boy

Question 18:
Who is first black man to hold the office of Mayor in Natchez, since Reconstruction?
A. George F. West Sr.
B. Philip West
C. George Harden
D. Michael Butler

Question 19:
How many people from Natchez were taken to Parchment (Mississippi State Penitentiary) for Parading Without A Permit in 1965?
A. 10
B. 200
C. 1000
D. 85

Question 20:
In what year did Rev. G.C. Ford of Natchez, Mississippi attend the 6th International UNIA Convention in Kingston, Jamaica?
A. 1919
B. 1905
C. 1929
D. 1935

ANSWERS

1. A The Bambara
2. C 1833
3. A George Metcalfe
4. B Rhythm Club
5. C Walter Barnes and Orchestra
6. B Zion Chapel A.M.E. Church
7. D William "Bill" Ware
8. A Louis Winston
9. B John R. Lynch
10. C Robert Wood
11. D 2015
12. A 1863
13. C 1968
14. D Both B & C
15. B University in Timbuktu
16. A Travis Patten
17. D Black Boy
18. B Philip West
19. B 200
20. C 1929

Thanks to the residents of Natchez, Miss Lou Heritage Group & Tours

Bryan Mcknight
Greg Robinson Jr.
Gregory Garcia
Shabilla Adams-Minor
Randy Minor
Sydni Adams
Symari Adams
Symone Adams
Sandra Johnson
Greg Myles
Gabrielle Day
Rufus "Bull" Wiley Jr.
Stephanie Dreher
Jennifer Hill
Paul Armstead Jr
Wharlest Jackson Jr
Denise Ford
Cedric King
Darrell White
Pastor Kevin Deason
Jarita F. King
Dorothy Sanders
Jason Clark
Ser Seshs Ab Heter-Boxley